VALENTINE'S DAY

Activity Book for Kids

*Mazes, Coloring and Puzzles
for kids Ages 4-8*

Young Scholar

All rights reserved. No part of this document may be reproduced Used or transmitted in any form or by any means, electronic or otherwise. This means you cannot photocopy any material ideas or tips that are provided in this book.

Young Scholar
Published by Ciparum LLC

Valentines Day Activity Book for Kids
© 2017 Ciparum LLC
All rights reserved.
ISBN-10:1-63589-199-X
ISBN-13:978-1-63589-199-7

My Name

Valentine's Day

Match the shadow to the right Cupid

Guide Cupids Arrow to the Heart

COLOR AND CUT

guide the hearts to the center

Answer on the next page

ANSWER:

COLOR ME!

DOT TO DOT
Connect the dots and color

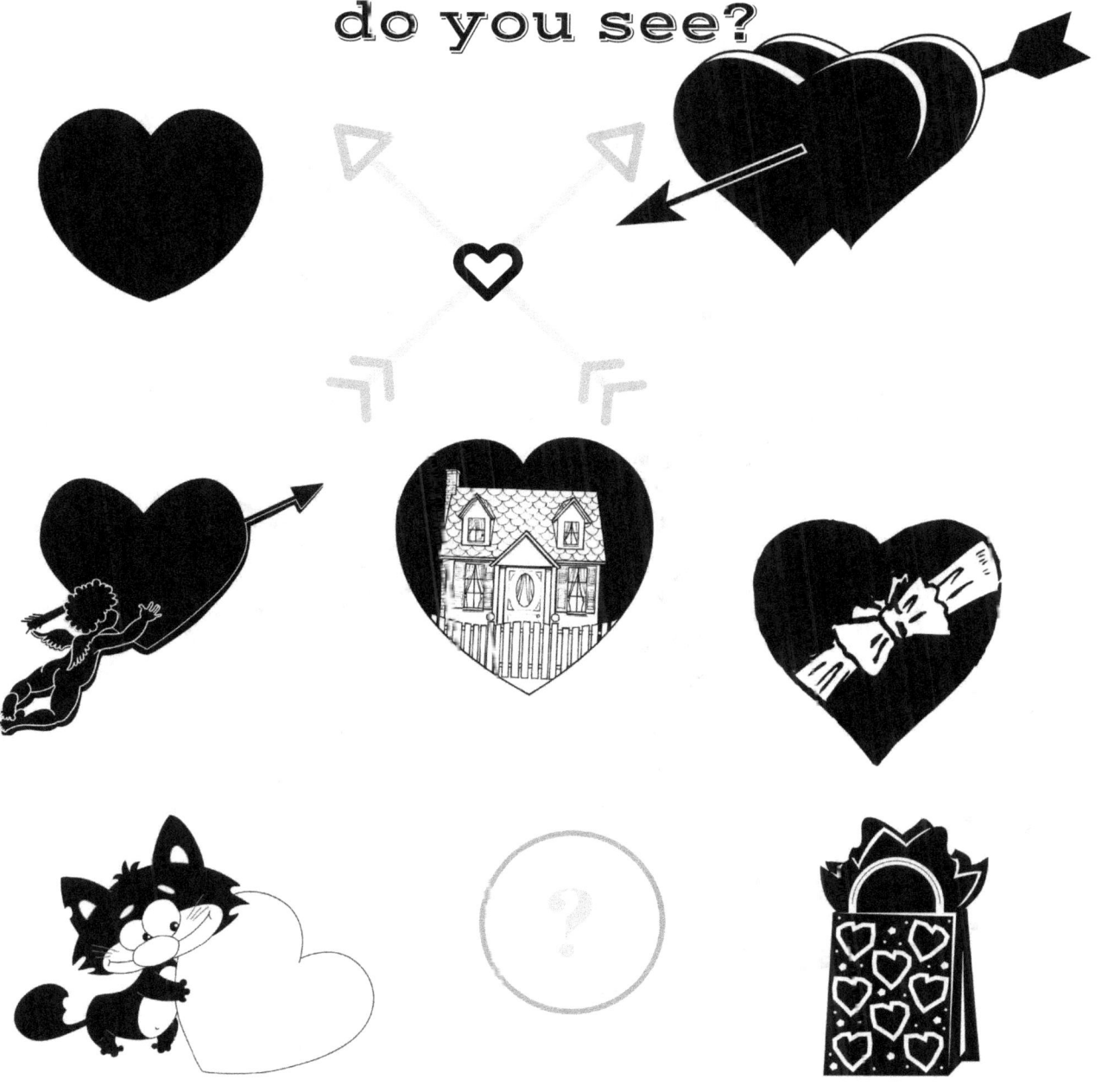

COLOR ME!

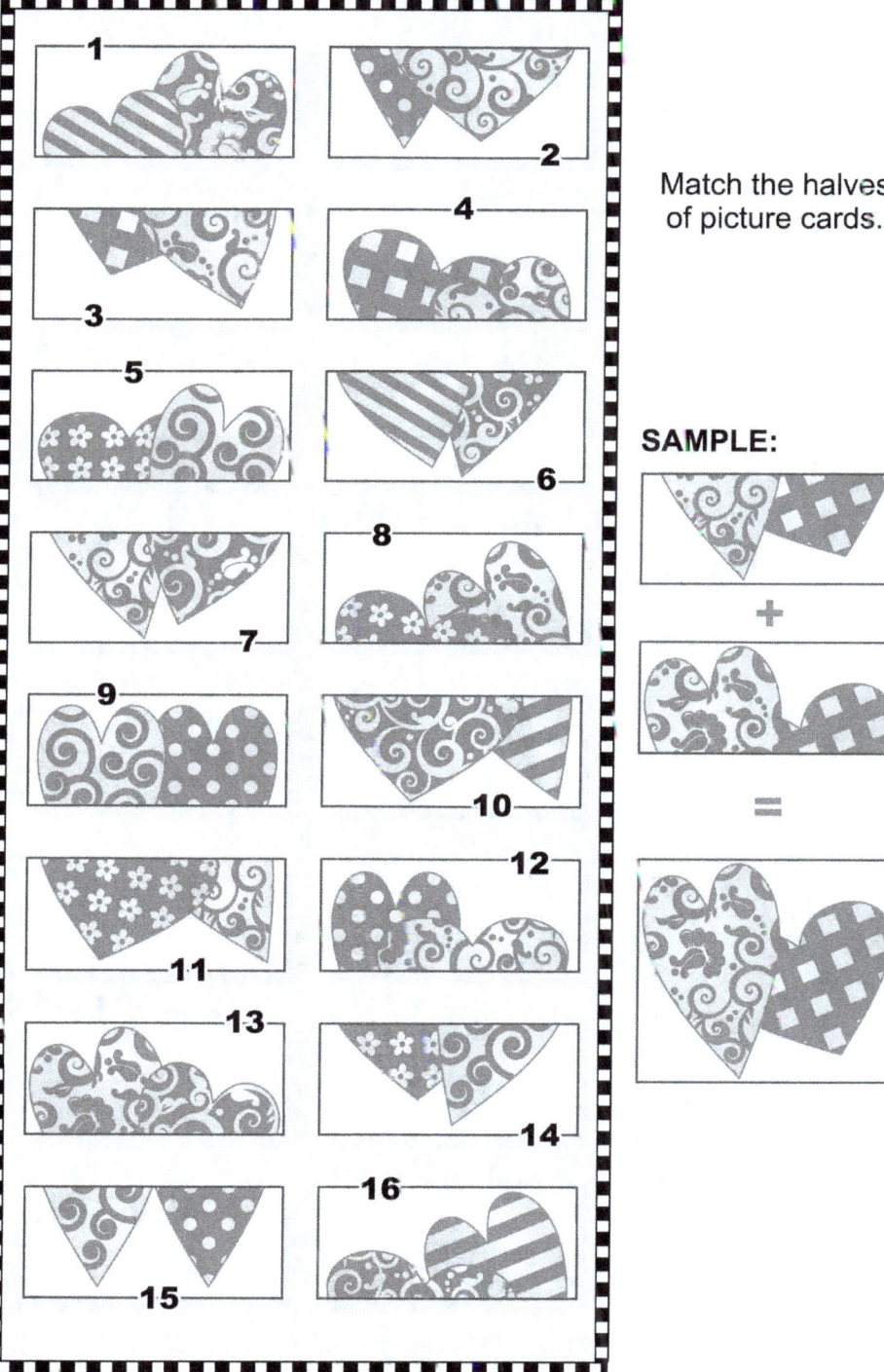

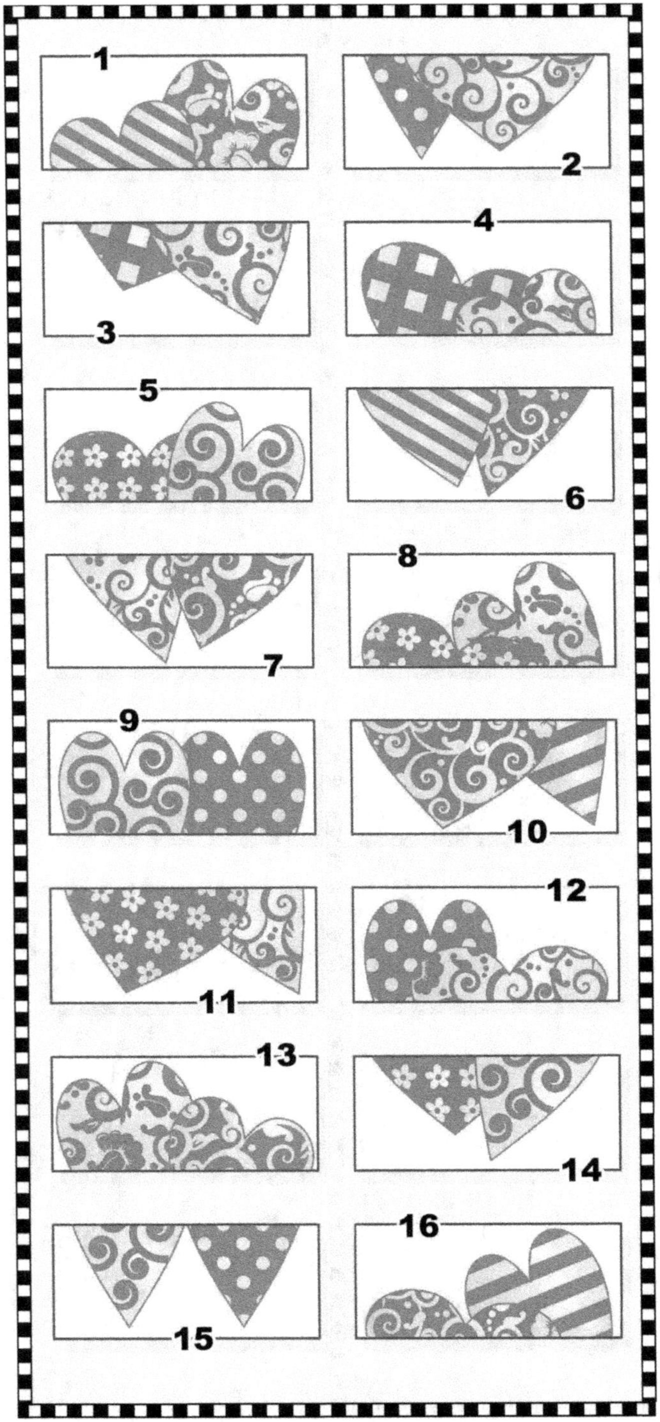

Match the halves of picture cards.

SAMPLE:

+

=

ANSWER:

1-6, 2-12, 3-4, 5-14, 7-13, 8-11, 9-15, 10-16.

connect the dots
cupid to teddy

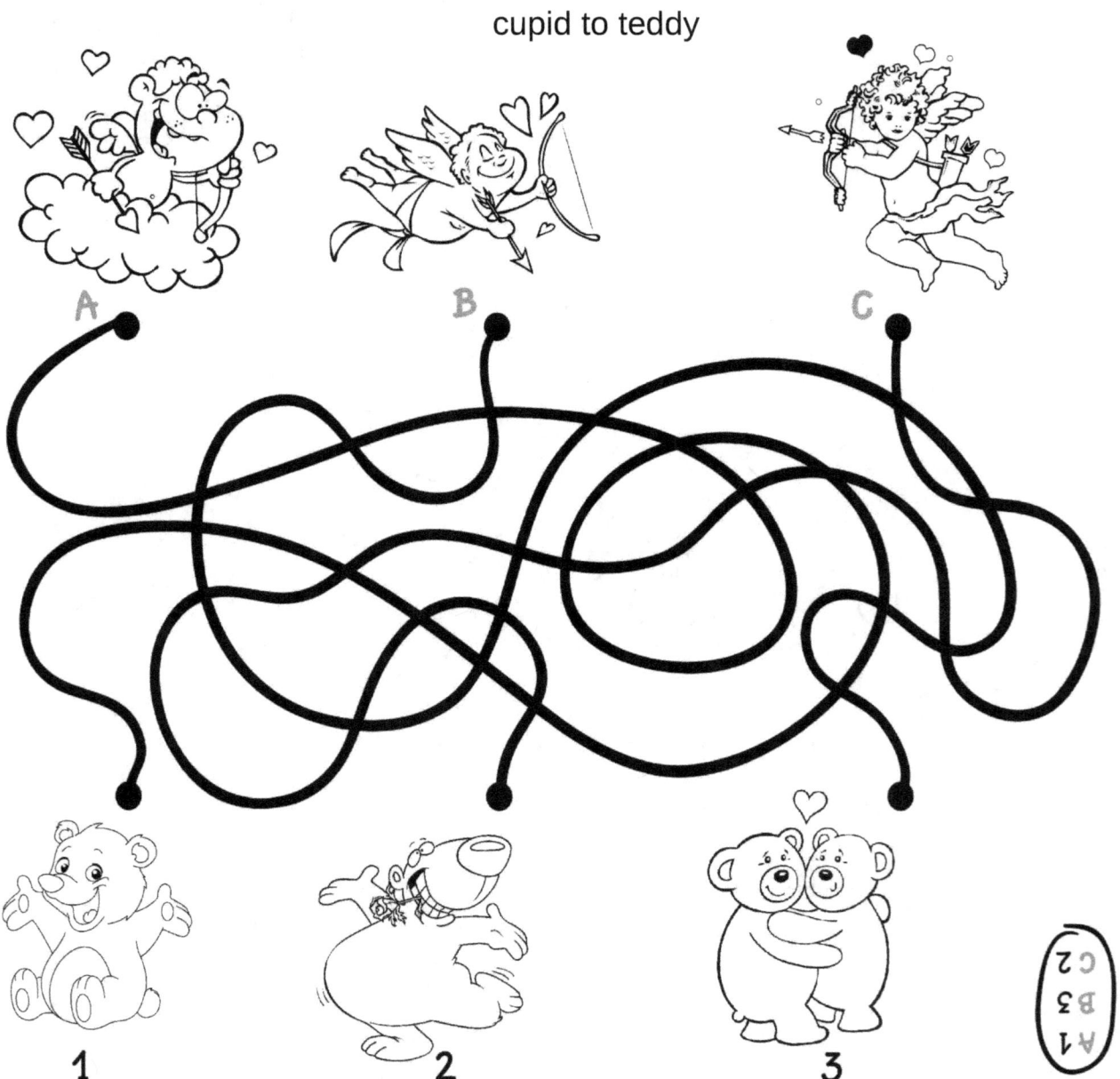

Dot to Dot

Connect the dots and color

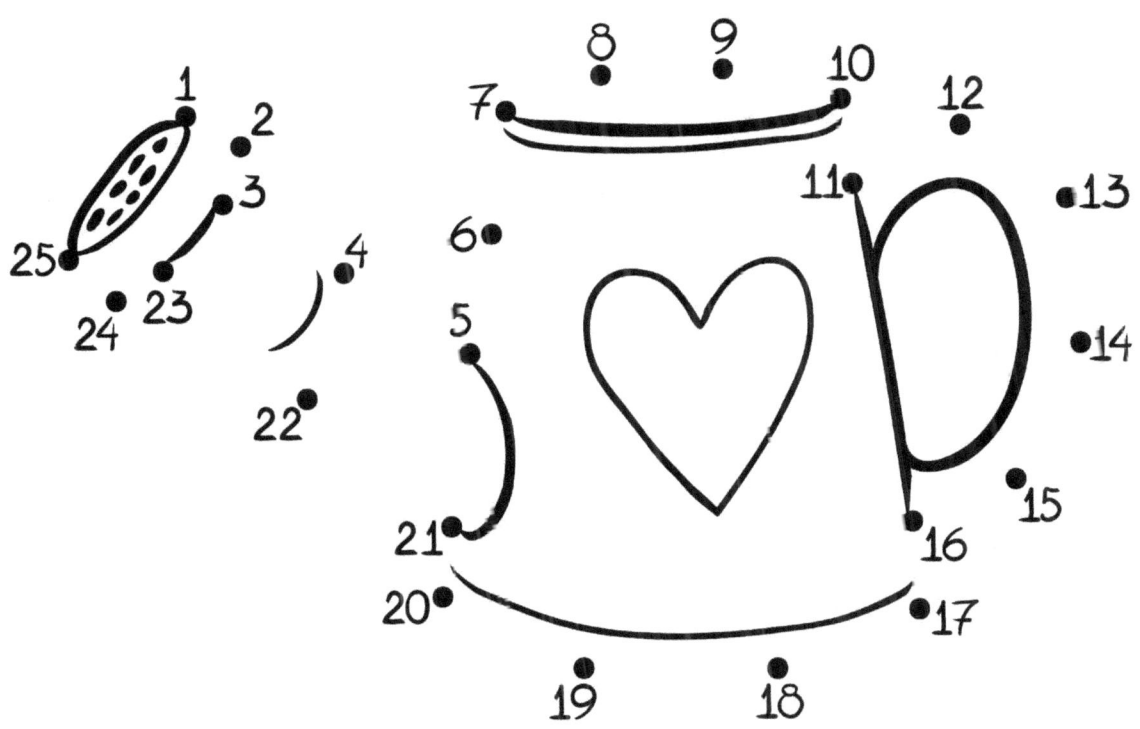

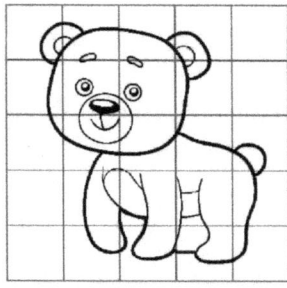

Grid draw

Use the grid as a guide and draw the image

PICTURE SUDOKU
Fill in the blanks using same hearts as the above set has.
When you finish, there should be only one of each heart in a row and in a column.

PICTURE SUDOKU
Fill in the blanks using same hearts as the above set has.
When you finish, there should be only one of each heart in a row and in a column.

ANSWER: 6-5, 7-3, 8-1, 9-4, 10-2, 11-4, 12-5.

MATCH EACH VALENTINE CUPCKAE TO ITS SHADOW

dot to dot
Connect the dots and color

Connect the dots

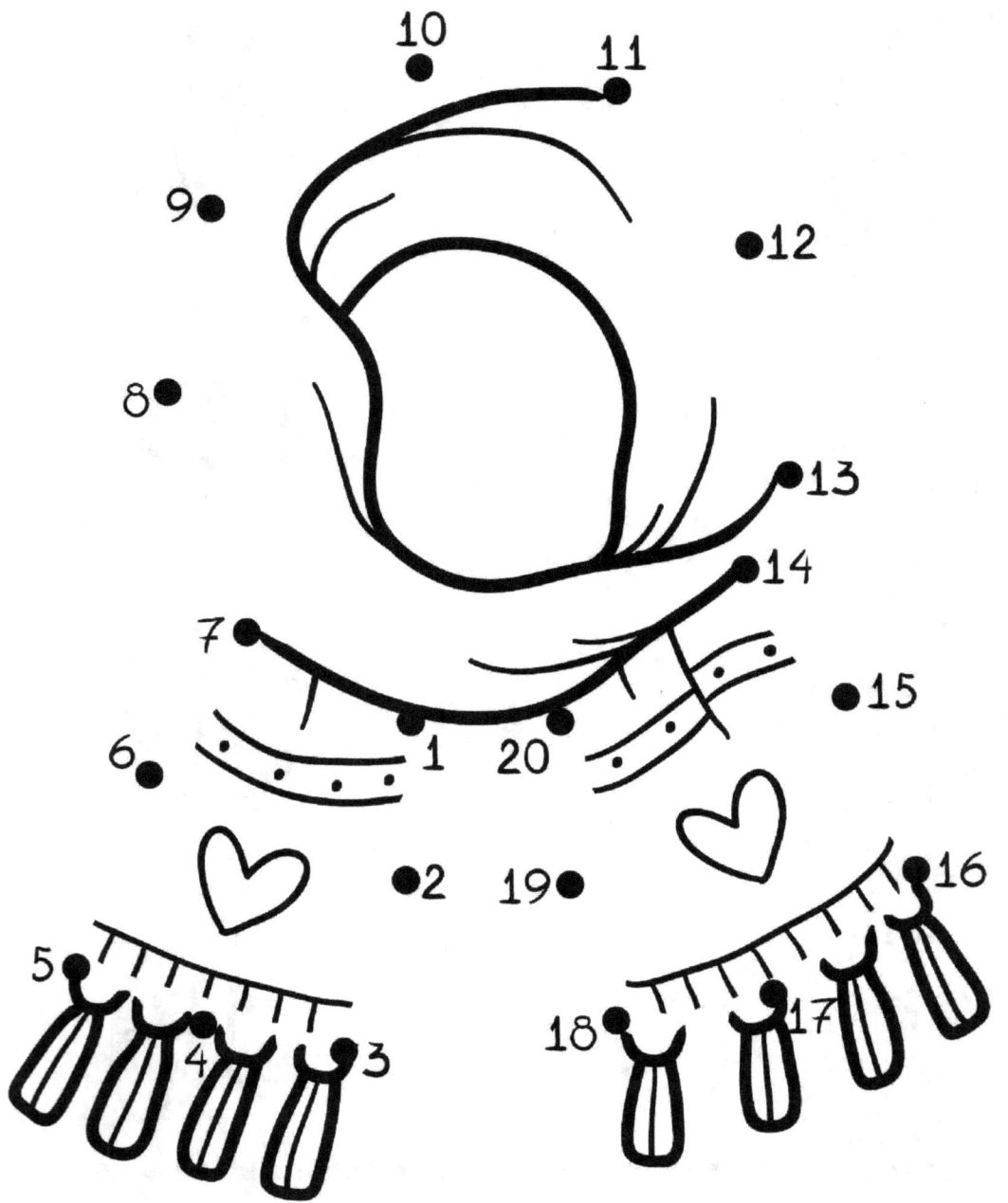

Help Cupid deliver the present

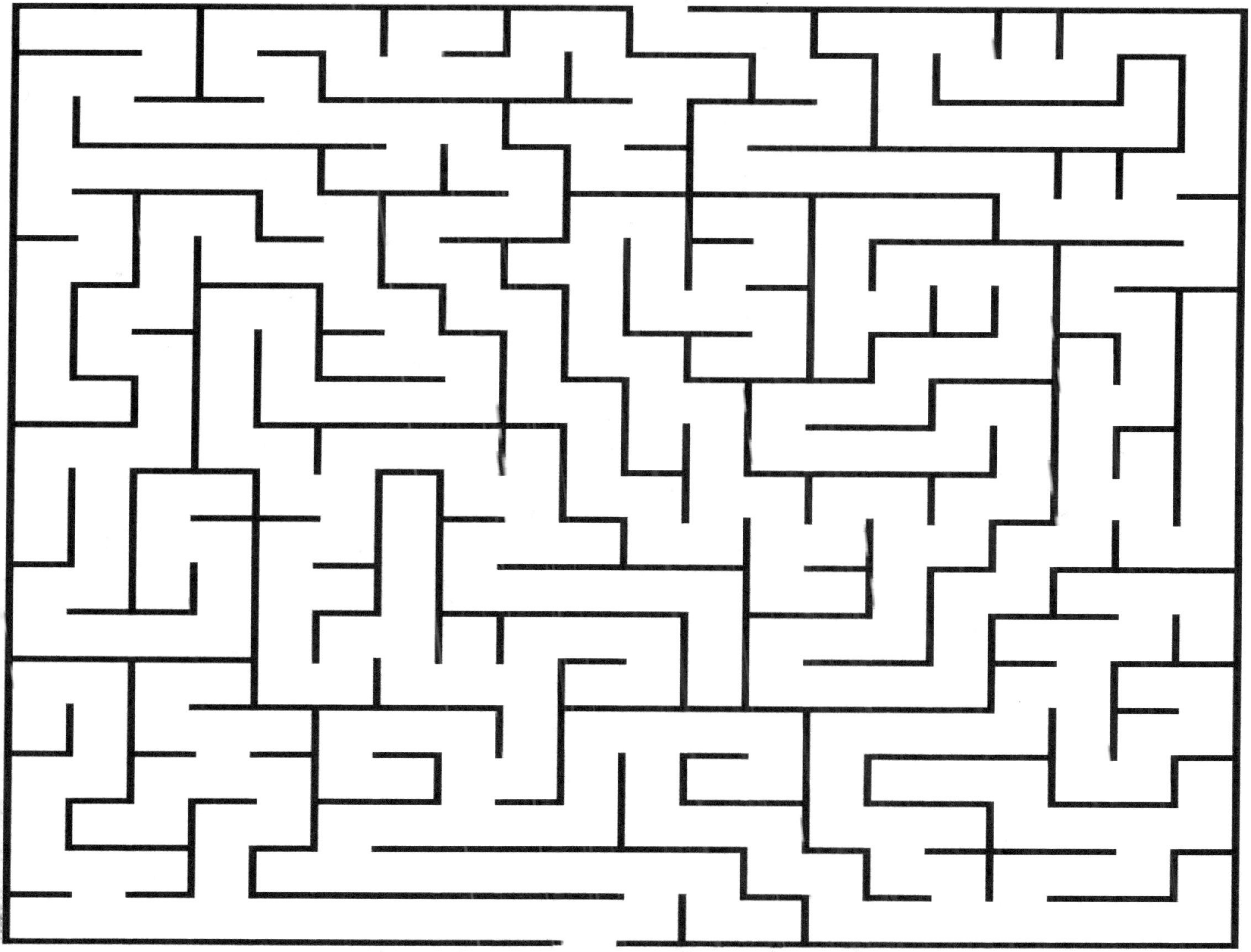

Dot to Dot

Connect the dots and connect

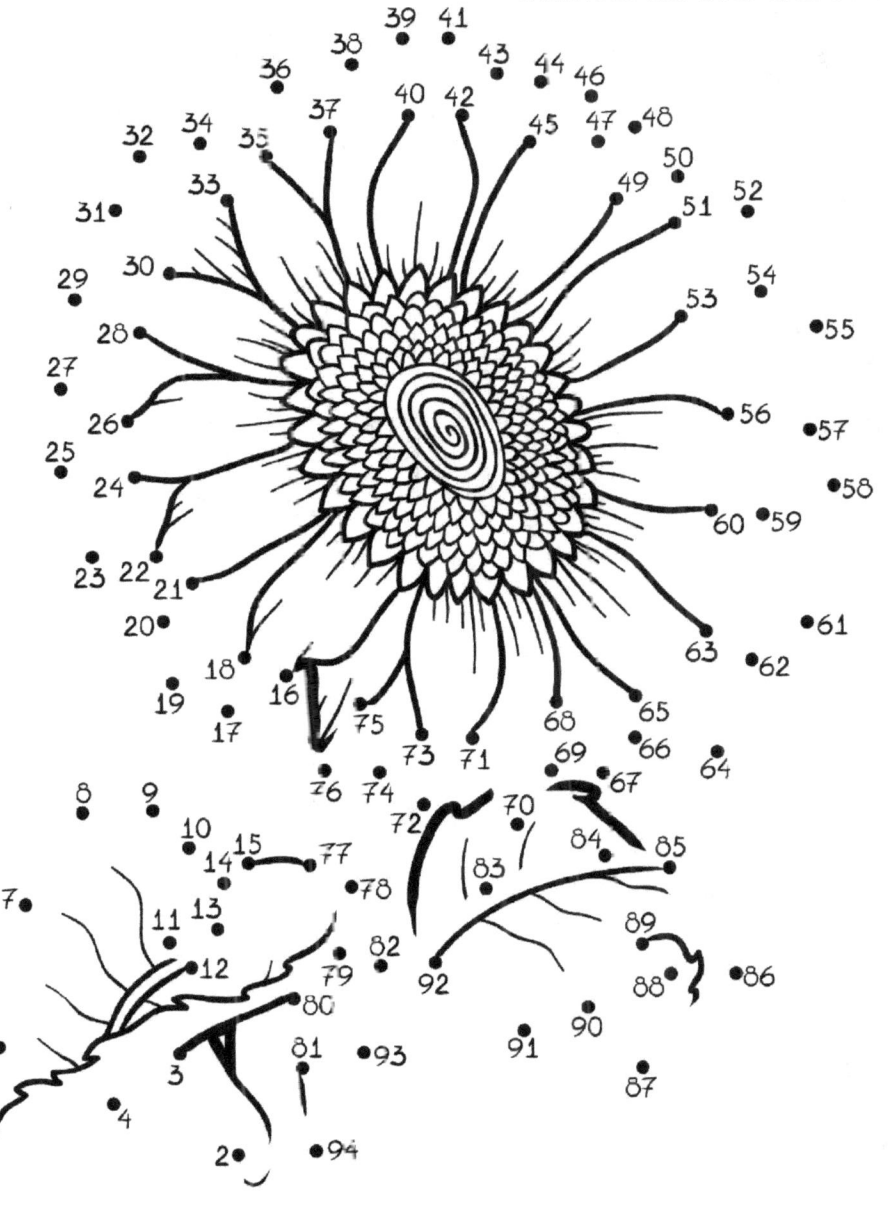

What is missing?
Fill in the missing alphabet

C _ P _ D

_ E _ _ Y _ E _ _

_ E _ _ T

COLOR ME!

www.ingramcontent.com/pod-product-compliance
Lightning Source LLC
Chambersburg PA
CBHW051429070526
44584CB00023B/3649